AF167690

A QUESTION OF GRAVITY

ELIZABETH SMITHER

A Question of Gravity

SELECTED POEMS

PUBLICATIONS

2004

Published by Arc Publications
Nanholme Mill, Shaw Wood Road
Todmorden OL14 6DA, UK

© Elizabeth Smither 2004

Design by Tony Ward
Print by Antony Rowe Ltd.,
Eastbourne, East Sussex

ISBN 1 900072 75 0

Cover photograph © Kate Mellor

Poems in this collection have
previously been pubished in
Shakespeare Virgins (AUP / OUP, 1983)
Professor Musgrove's Canary (AUP / OUP, 1986)
A Pattern of Marching (AUP, 1989)
The Tudor Style: poems new & selected (AUP, 1993)
The Lark Quartet (AUP, 1999)
Red Shoes (Godwit, 2003)

The Publishers acknowledge financial
assistance from ACE Yorkshire

Arc Publications International Poets
Series Editor: John Kinsella

for Barbara Ewing

Contents

Girl and wolfhound at Glebe

So might it be titled in a painting
deep-framed in gold summer light
and underneath a little polished plaque:
Girl and her wolfhound at Glebe.

Take out the crass crossing lights
that hold them momentarily together
stilled as the artist always wishes
creating the subject onto which to shimmer

the pale near-transparent long white dress
loose-hanging below the elaborate braided hair
into which – what artifice! – small crystals
wink and glitter. And the wolfhound, so

rumpled, shaggy, half-depleted of his fur
except that is his style – as if he's just risen
from lying uncombed at his mistress's feet
and is instantly on the lookout for wolves

of the suburban variety. His leash
hangs in her gentle hand, an arc.
He half-wanders, being too royal to succumb
to any command other than her poise.

A dentist's view of heaven

No drill, no syringes, no mouth washes
no cotton wadding like tiny bolsters
no excavating a tooth like a collapsed

house in which at the bottom remains
like a family safe in a doodlebug bombing
a base of still-living tooth.

And no conversation either: the
one-sided memoir of Dentistry School
the fearsome lecturers, themselves like molars

or Dracula teeth. The wearing of surgical gloves
from the beginning. The question at the interview:
Why do you want to be a dentist? to which

his honest reply troubled: *Because it's more
secure* than his first love: astrophysics.
Nothing gets completed in this life, we agree

as the injection takes hold, sealing off
sections of gum and cheek, side of tongue.
In which case, in a completed heaven, he'll

have a simple wand. Just go around
touching it to the side of jaws that ache
miraculously completing caps with a tap

inserting back lost teeth held in milk
or ice, like in the poster in the waiting room
No more gaps. Flying and loved

not like the dread statistics that say
translation for dentists is a strong possibility
but loved and loved, a special angel.

To Fiona, in memory of Flora

And in a deathly sleep rest thousands of footsteps –
Akhmatova's line – and now your dear mother
grown so small and frail but so spirited
lays her footsteps over the others

and you see them, leading back, and forwards
into your life to come, for mothers
relinquish nothing that is their children's
even eternity is a place to step through

on hot coals if need be or ice
that cracks and shatters. Nothing deters
that bent determined head, the gaze
of eyes, so true and truthful.

O let petals from fallen roses in vases
be lain quickly over her little footprints
before another comes, let them be perfumed
and especially light and joyful.

Eating oranges

Soft-skinned pipless oranges
whose peel makes small dishes
of clotted cream and under-glow

eating one or two is enough
to conjure a treeful and some
fallen on the green grass around

and a life of not merely fruit
with discarded skins but books
open and lyres flung

as if opening is all treasure
on some supporting ground:
a table, a chair with shawl.

Borrowing a bed

My best bed to… my hose
bequeathed to… Queen Bess
slept here on her progress to…
refreshed horses, refreshed Queen rode off

and the bed curtains were beaten
the sheets boiled and put to dry
the air in four-posters must be haunted by
dreams piled up like the cemetery at Versailles

so when I borrow a neighbour's bed
– admittedly single, no curtains –
I'm still awed by the solidity of the thing
being borrowed and the weight of sleeping in it.

North light and lip pencil

The cruellest light that makes
as it traverses the face a tome
of disasters like a crumbling stone.

Even a name this light withdraws.
But wait. The fine lip pencil draws
where the flaws would reach a line

a Cupid-shaped dyke, a hope
that north light artifice will wane
from fine confidence defined.

A poem for Roseanne

Roseanne who cuts my hair
every six weeks and asks
How's your hair been?
as if hair was my life

belongs to a rowing club
goes rowing in an eight
all pretty girls with hair
in the latest cuts and shades.

While Roseanne cuts my hair
I imagine her on a lake
in the middle of a rowing eight
keeping a perfect stroke.

The starter lies down on the dock
and holds the prow in place
the cox is so encased
she could be a coffined dwarf.

And then Roseanne and the rest
put all their strength to their stroke
Roseanne puts my hair in place
and the boat shoots through the water.

Stars through tree crowns

How perfectly and with such a leap
the leaves become stars, the stars'
leaf-fall that levitates, not falls.

How surrounded we are all the time
by frames we are unaware of
the huge tree crowns, the so-distant stars.

The gleam and glow of one in starlight
falling on their heads, the fallen light
lifting again to the severe source

like the puzzling condescension of God
so hard to explain: such distance between
the light and the light's work.

Tree breath and human

Trees in the garden are expelling
the breath I need. It enters windows
and I breathe out what they breathe in.

How we should love them, never moving
from their posts, withstanding wind
creaking sometimes, losing limbs

but aiding us with oxygen.
While we climb them to gulp in
the freshest air, the most pure

reason for their being here:
their breath and ours commingling
into needful dependencies.

Leaf on leaf

Onto a large platelike leaf
a smaller leaf has fallen
and rests there held by the curvature
the slight suction of drying rain
the pressing down of wind.

How charming if all trees were
similarly double-paged. As if
each message held a smaller billet-doux
each spoken word cupped another
sotto voce, translating itself further.

An arborist at work

Rope-supported, spike-booted
in the dead tree, chain saw hanging
alarmingly like a lemur's tail

the tree he feels himself into –
this one needs extra care with toeholds
since death has already taken

blossoms and leaf, blackened the bark
like blue fingers on the dying –
begins, once the canopy is gone

in a series of quick judicious incisions
to resemble a building or a ship
in which the arborist clings to the funnel

and cuts not merely the tree but himself
down to ground level, as if in a column
of air he has descended from space.

This new-found light and space
weighs on his shoulders as he comes down
branch by branch, footstool trunk.

Hearing the approach of rain

Waking as it begins: the light
rush of rain through a little grove
not deep but with substantial trees
and spaces, a real undergrowth
in which, nearer dawn, wild cries
of something fleeing from pursuit

rise up. Just sufficient trees
to make the passage of rain through them a
unique exercise. Premonition,
sound, movement, actuality, all one
and to hear it, suddenly, out of
dark silence, an unwrapped gift.

A whole day's rain

For hours now it's been a habit:
the first welcoming drops
have settled into 'steady' drizzle
two terms that don't quite add up

as if one could cry for hours
in rhythm. Without hiccups
or drawing in air in great lungfuls
the better to continue. Not that

but gently like an upended river
seeping from a top floor to a basement
or someone pouring, biting their lip,
water from a clear jug to a flower.

Gallimaufry

for Viv

Okay, here's the word for the day.
No cheating by looking in the dictionary.
Gallimaufry: what is it?
You leave a slip of paper on my desk.

I cheat of course. But the inferior dictionary
I first consult is watered and weak.
I come downstairs. You're near the *Oxford*.
I don't know, I have to confess.

And yet it stirs before you know it.
Something stirs: is it elephants
and the way they walk, their tiny tails
close brackets of their awesome trunks?

Or parrots in trees so high above
their colours shock and startle?
Perhaps a dish of unlikely combinations
definitely with shellfish and a coloured sauce?

How that mysterious word rises and dips
superior up to *ll* and then a swamp
or a broken-backed bed
the end: a positively clerical curlicue.

Severe as some music starting in the strings
then surprised by a low deep grumble
a masculine plaint of silence and romance
the need to put on a good surface cover.

We sit in the bus together going home.
Gallimaufry, you explain, will be
the name of your next house:
a jumble, hotch-potch, and on the stove a ragout.

Wave on a speckled sea

A surface flecked with pointillism
not the pointillism of squints and shaded eyes
but endless equally-spaced wave-incorporated flecks

which the wave wears while it breathes
as a human might wear a scar, a burn
but feel internally unchanged.

Only to the eye is there difference:
an existence and its normal mechanics overlaid
with eye-absorbing all-cancelling design

as if design breathes above sea breath
or human breath, as fleck on neighbouring fleck
semaphores delight in its own text.

Storm in a little bay

Everything moves in a chopping motion
the waves like wood splinters rise and fall
the air is full of anguished particles
the sand blows, grass flattens, trees whip

yet everything is in perfect accord
cause and effect never came so close
chop and splinter and particle
the air like a simultaneous translation

see and see and see how
divided makes more homogeneity
each individually rises by applause
into this windy alert spotlight.

Standing by the sea with Tonia

Tennyson's sea must have been narrow
for his thoughts to rise and be
his and sufficiently his.

This sea before us is so high and wide
the great grey embankment stones
will surely be nibbled down.

Instinctively we know to go on speaking
sure our ordinary but wondering conversation
has a place in this literature.

Irene's spa

In swimsuits, since the city is so close
(though we look down on it it might look up)
we sit in the spa pool like a cup

of blue water or a tiny lake
enclosed in a room with window panes
and young growing vines, again –

we do it every time I visit –
skirting subjects which remain
deep and blue and plain

as our bodies' elongated reflections.
My white toes stretch out and glow
our lives surround us, enclosed

in a compass, we circumnavigate
to turn the bubbles on or off
say it's too hot or not.

Three women sharing a bowl
of *crème brûlée*

In a small brown pudding bowl
with a syrup-coloured stripe
on a brown base plate

our three spoons scoop.
'One *crème brûlée, s'il vous plaît*
and three dining-with-the-devil spoons.'

One indivisible glacé cherry
at the centre like a navel
how unsophisticated in a sophisticated

restaurant to have just one
surviving appetite after the appetiser
a glass of house white

and two compatriots press-ganged
into something they've never conceived:
burnt cream. Culinary accidents

the culinary leader speaks of
that upended tart with apples
dropped on the hot plate by a furious

overheated woman named Tatin
or crêpes Suzette accidentally designed
by someone half-pickled

accidents which on the instant of occurring
or in culinary terms – combining – become
a poet's inspired instinctive metre

a villanelle perhaps, an enjambment
so full of joy its creation
resembles wind through the open window.

'Satisfactory?' The waiter goes past
peers in the bowl where spoons
keep returning over faint protests

'I'm not really hungry but I can't resist.'
'You have the cherry. It was your idea.'
And as the last crumbs of the crust

are tenderly scraped we seem to be
wrapping the crying Tatin in a shawl
and setting her in a rocker, bringing brandy

or toasting crêpes Suzette with more brandy
deliriously clinking glasses until we swoon
over the tablecloth in huge top-heavy hats.

At a gallery

for Tonia

'Is that old man you know who?'
you said looking down over
the gallery balcony at a view
of a thinning pate. 'Truly?'

Would he say looking at us: 'Those two
though carefully made up show
around their necks the touch of crepe
and keep their hands well out of sight'?

But mostly it is the balcony I enjoy
leaning against it with wider waists
'You have a waist still!' you exclaimed
embracing me with an old friend's frisk

as if we were in the police. How good
the balcony felt that afternoon
as if everything that had ever passed
had been in a different kind of air

and now, we ourselves, were art
walking equably between the exhibits
stepping back, or peering at a name
giving everything our wise consideration.

Thomas Chambers, *Niagara Falls*
(Nineteenth-century American),
The Wadsworth Athenaeum, Hartford

In the catalogue it looked less primitive:
a man in moleskins stood on a rock
a forking branch emerged from the water
and the falls fell like a white horse tail

but now it's arrived in its cylinder
I see there are mistakes made in perspective
and it's one of those paintings which
the purchaser purchases to forgive the artist

and provide a comment. 'I was there in '86
and thought this amusingly captured it.
The man in moleskins was nowhere in sight
but helicopters circled looking for barrels:

a repeated student practice. We rode
The Maid of the Mist into the mist
and here, modestly, like the artist I faltered
and thought it was rain wetting my face

or some cloudburst above roaring.'
So now I better understand the painting
the man with no footfall in sight
and the water pouring and pouring.

Winslow Homer's *The New Novel*, Museum of Fine Arts, Springfield, Massachusetts

Only a poster and a portrait of a book
that someone's lying sideways to read
an orange faded front-buttoning dress
an orange hip, black buttons, collar and cuffs

orange hair that's straggling on a rug
that's orange stripe-bisected too
and orange hose disappearing into one shoe.
The colour of late summer on the grass

the palest faintest green with orange gleams
as if the sun has rusted. A few clover leaves
a few long stalks of grass before a hedge
fills the whole somnolent background in.

The end of a garden perhaps? Somewhere
no interruption will come. The cushioned head
the book just the right distance to show
fine sight. Fine thought being taken in

because the expression has that suspension
we expect art to provide. Not kicks.
The features half-look as if they could slip
except the book holds them enthralled

and when, eventually, the hip begins to ache
the reader will roll over on her back
and hold the book across her breast
to sleep off the memories it's brought.

The Lark Quartet

for Beth

Four larks on an unseasonal evening
from their first notes made spring
from wands and deep low cello bowing
like a river under a subway.

New York, we said later. Those tenements
that yet give shelter to bold animals
the russet tail by the dustbin, the birds
of common breed but rare tenacity

and Mozart, following, reminded you of
wallpaper. Someone heaving up resolve
to begin another room, scoured by stains.
Definitely a sense of 'here we go again'

in which after weariness came mastery.
The unavoidable good performance we discussed
later over cake and coffee. Once started
Mozart invariably knew where he was going:

into misunderstood pauperism. Shostakovich
wrestled like a chill wind just above the ground
a height so hard to obliterate or fold
into conformity. Last what we understood

most easily: a dance, a movement of folk tunes.
Disharmonies crossed over them like light showers
but we were at our ease now with how
the melody is greatest shown to emerge

a bow's hair ahead of its sound of birth.
We are a generation of assemblers
who want the miracle not quite clear
but tuned to our attention and our inattentiveness.

Now I could confess I admired the shoes
of the first violinist and craned to see
through some notes' pictures if the others
were similarly shod. And you could swear

the beautiful nape of the one with short hair
and her strong straight spine, glowing cummerbund
in gold and red and silver embroidery
was just exquisite going through the curtain.

Singing hymns

The only time the voice makes a bell
and moves from bell to bell
being both the bellringer and the aperture
high in the bell tower through which
the bell note sounds across the fields

as if a monk pulling on the rope
ran suddenly up a flight of spiral stairs
leaning into the tower's coil and caught
the pure outpouring as it issued
pure and yet drowned in other bells.

A woman on a bus reading a poem

Not just a poem but a long
sinuous spinelike coiling down the page
the strong spine of the long poem!

Only in a long poem do the margins retreat
like someone wiping their lips with a white serviette
at a banquet, outdoors, under clouds.

And the courage it takes to read one!
Has this woman checked out what she's in for
the long haul of page after page

through which the thought runs
picking images like orchard fruit
musing, giving little bits away

soliciting interest as fishes on the ocean floor
solicit divers weighted with lead
aware always of interest flagging

unless with the purposefulness of a river
before the next meander's due
the reader's allowed an uninterrupted view.

Two pages turn. The eyes scan down.
A heroine in a bus proceeds
like an angel above machinery.

A television image of looters

Coming out of the looted emporium
onto the street which always seems to have
a raised pavement, deep gutters

stepping through the glass like diamonds
like angels departing a tomb
holding a basketful of items

or simply one possession in one hand
how many seem to wear in spite of
the danger, the imminent fires, the explosions

the innocent expression associated with statuary
with blank eyes, as if, if they could find
somewhere in this teeming crush a garden

they would turn into statues with one arm aloft
a sword, a parchment, a book and pen
and grow quiet to the sound of a fountain.

Cycle race

High above the city a siren sounds
then a yellow car is located travelling
fast along a Sunday street.

Now comes a marvellous thing:
a line of left-handed brackets
(((((((((((((one behind the other.

These are the cyclists, bending
over their handlebars, backs
curved like the sun on their wheel rims

trying to catch up to the siren
which will be impaled on a straight line
they will cross, a dash————————————

A man walking in white shoes

From a panoramic window seat
overlooking scores of streets I watch
the distant walking of white feet.

A man in white sandshoes follows a curve
on a grey pavement, a grey road
around which his white swollen feet go.

White swells, grey shrinks. His feet magnified
make walking magnificent. Entranced
I watch white doves rise and dip

or someone reverently handling plates
two white minims on stave-like legs
making that section of the road so sweet

to walk around a curve in white shoes seems
worth calling an angel down to peer
at motion made so pure and clear.

A stone armadillo

for Sarah

Who would not love an ideal creature
conveyed to stone? A family 'intermediate
between the sloths and the anteaters'
with a 'variation of simple molars interlocking
when the mouth is shut'. Stone bands

stone flakes imitate the shields and plates
that encase them as they move by night
in a range between Texas and Patagonia.
From Texas you wrote: I can hear the armadillos
crashing through the undergrowth like myself

at summer camp. Armadillos became the
common word in letters. Any more sightings
of those adorable warriors whose persisting
became your leitmotif? They eat better
than the campers: worms, roots, fruit

and insects. By day they burrow as we
lolled beside the pool after trekking.
Some homesick girls cried. The armadillos
crashed night after night as if pushing aside
another Texan day. Many died in flight

caught in headlights or drowned. I lift
the stone armadillo in my arms and
almost fall into a pile of Aladdin pots.
Too dear to purchase legitimately I'd like to
steal back at night, smash glass, and grab

the dear creature for the garden. Have you round
far from Texas now to view. There's a strange
creature just appeared, perhaps you can identify?
And on its stone ridges leaves would catch
rain stain and, like travel, evaporate again.

A cast iron miniature stove

Wouldn't you prefer a piece of tartan?
ask my relatives as we trudge
up and down the Royal Mile

but there's tartan enough in the air
to clothe a blackened church for winter
to tie bows on every lamppost

instead I'd like this little cast iron stove
primitive and utilitarian as porridge
with a chimney stack and oven

worked like an assiduous steam train
coal glowing through it like a Presbyterian heart
which must produce to feel righteous

and all the scouring that must have followed
the soaking pots, the heavy frypan
the ashes dumped, the blacking

to set the heart for another rising
the little iron door that clangs shut
like a cold bank vault over frivolous filigree.

A teacup with floral decoration

On the side that faces me
the full-blown flower waves
and is zoomed over by a butterfly.

I lift it to my mouth and touch
the purplish flower: *meadow cranesbill*.
My throat reflects its undershine

like the game of holding buttercups
under the chin. The hot tea burns
inside its tube like the flower's stem.

On the side that faces away
the flower is in autumn and Latin
Geranium pratense: frail and final.

The little graveyard

On the slope of a little hill
where one might roll down
then pluck straws and
decorously open a book

lie graves in a sweet opened palm
in unmown summer grass

the colour of summer hats
with posies at their throats.

No more than twenty rolling down
and coming to rest in a heap
divided by limbs and petticoats
lying languorously on their backs.

From a ha-ha to a cemetery

for Beth and David

How wise to have this unseen ditch between
our present basking in spring air and
the end. The lines on lines of beloved books
or beds of stone that climb the hill
and pause at a vista with a yew

or obelisk, a cross on the horizon
that's surely not contrived but by being placed
draws the eye into an accent and wonderment.
How envious I think I am of this
holding and focusing your binoculars

when a black dog bounds into view
or a little party comes, dressed in pale colours
to examine and then surround
a minister with a Bible. I hold their stillness
in the glass, hardly breathing. Only the words

are absent. Not ha-ha obviously but
beloved, that strange deadened word
that covers like an eiderdown
all failings in a nest of feathers.
No one here is not beloved or missed

and if they rose would be instantly kissed
like Lazarus by his sisters or set down
to eat and drink as we are on the lawn.
I pass the binoculars back. The group
breaks up, the dog, unconcerned, bounds
across beloved, beloved and beloved.

A death and a marriage in one day

I put on a huge black hat
which looks out of place as if
I'm in *fin de siècle* Paris
leaning on a white tablecloth.

All those black and white stripes surely
hinted at unconcealable death
all those fixed eyes and despairing smiles
grown dark in watchful corners.

All those vows and then no vow left
but a life of making one long joined
vow of everything, complete and incomplete
all those hats and flowers.

The announcement of a pregnancy

The tentative voice that asked
if a schoolfriend could stay overnight
or help be given with a project

now in the woman requires consent:
I'm pregnant. No soft way to announce
except in the soft wondering words: *I'm pregnant*

and instantly the congratulations like a stream
seek to express themselves. When and have you been
for confirmation yet? No need yet

she says: I took a test. A frog? But no
poor sacrificed frogs for golden moments are gone.
Some chemicals have changed colour. What wonders

and when the phone is dead the day seems golden
as if every bit of winter sun doubles to bless
its chores, to gild the announcement with the moment.

Sarah in the second trimester

Her navel's reversed – good for cleaning
and a wall seems to be growing, front and sides
a thickening like grain stored in a tower.

The glowing trimester – I'm looking forward
all that activity and the stillness of sunlight
caressing gratuitously the pattern perfect

gilding the baroque: more gold leaf
and more, acorns and grapes and even
the gargoyles rendered innocuous.

A woman watching cricket

No woman will ever commentate
even if she is fluent in the positions
or be let into the secret of how
they remove the red ball stains from trousers.

It is enough for her to see
and applaud in the right places
white men on a green field
over a brown crease like a parting.

Even if she can pick a spinner
and understands about boxes, cover drives
and can tell a six before the signs go up
or the umpire performs hieroglyphics.

There are no women to replace the covers
when it rains though rain is a player
as anyone knows and as powerful
as any number of openers.

There will never be a woman commentator called Blowers
who says 'My dear young thing'
and puts a hand on a white thigh
and goes off to lunch in the pavilion.

The red brick quad

The ivy and the mullioned windows
are a slide rule over a sort of
atrium filled with creeper.
There is pride in your voice as you say
'Like one of the famous English colleges.'
I can see it is not. Something else

quite beautiful like the atom splits
in a cupboard among strewn paper
or a rose crawls through the window of the dissection lab.

The smile of the sweet-stall boy

Scales of justice levitate
as he knocks out Portia
with a day-long grin

or the Statue of Liberty
rests in his hand
the size and texture of a Mars bar.

Around the square of his stall
fountains and green spaces
with birds flying through the water.

Fr Anselm Williams and Br Leander Neville
hanged by Lutheran mercenaries in 1636 while
out of their monastery on a local errand
of charity – *from the guidebook to Ampleforth
Abbey and College*

'We'll see who can stick
their tongue out first for God
out of you two,' binding the hands
the flowers in the hedgerows starting
the sky turning over with a lurch
as when Brother Leander dropped the eggs.

They wouldn't be back to Compline.
The hedgeroses looked askance now.
A swallow passed. Their hands touched
just the fingertips like passing a note.
The tongues would come out later
into an air gone blue, a world.

The Tudor style

Katherine Howard practising
graceful poses for the block
ordering the block to her cell
like trying on a hat.

Violence and style together
violence in style the creed
that took them from bowls or tennis
to be served up like meat.

Would Henry get to hear of
the way Katherine Howard walked
how she disposed her neck, her skirts?
Unlikely: he was violently out

late partying, to correspond
with equal violence of forgetfulness
returning late down the river
after a day violently preoccupied

while all over the kingdom
games until the summons
were absorbingly violent, calmly
violent, graciously violently going on.

The family name

From Boston my mother gets
an envelope marked Hurry
send by return post your subscription
for a family history of the Harringtons.

Once it was a minor castle
near the Lake District needing donations
the demesne of a knight and lady
whose pile threatened to tumble.

In Northants once we found
a knee-high signpost: *Harrington*
in front of which we posed, two scions
in a ditch, travelling cross-country.

But my favourite Harringtons are
the two mentioned by Jane Austen
in *Pride and Prejudice*, Chapter 39
who, without any detail, sound pleasant.

Visiting Juliet Street

All the streets are named after Shakespeare.
Hamlet and Juliet are separated by an intersection
down which floats Ophelia Street, very sleepy.
They are all such demanding people
which lends the town an air of tragedy
as though Mercutio coming home after a party
failed to dip his lights and ran over
Polonius Street right up onto the sidewalk.
Even Shakespeare thought it best to keep them separated.
At the end of long girlish Juliet Street
with limbs like Twiggy the air grows
sleepier and sleepier as though
Juliet had anorexia nervosa and could hardly bear
a morsel of blossoms or any sap.

Swimming

THE MEETING OF OCEAN AND AIR

Of all the beautiful equal edges
which are everywhere observed: the edge
of this plank decking and the air for instance,
a leaf edge/air, an air/wing of bird,

this bubbling, live, taut, vivacious edge
of underwater ocean's edge and air
is the best example to be immersed in
to open eyes in and ride to surface.

Where else can be so graphically illustrated
how, in what manner, two elements meet
like Stanley and Livingstone, only better
for this handshake goes on for the length of a beach

and all around the world is transmitted
to anyone surfacing: a diver, a fish
a porpoise, an inept swimmer, gasping
streaming in the streaming that overcomes

even the fear of drowning: this perfect
sharp, soft, limber, rigorous, two-doctrine edge
like the Pope and the Dalai Lama meeting
under dissolving mosques and steeples and bells.

SWIMMING IN A SHOAL OF LITTLE FISH

We swim with our heads out and this shoal
of little fish does likewise: mouths and eyes
above the water, mouths that seem
tipped in plastic like umbrella ferrules.

It's late afternoon: mist and light rain
and the soft grey tide hardly swells.
The little shoals of fish embroider the shallows
like pins placed by serious seamstresses.

41

Swimming among them – it is impossible
to be eyeball to eyeball with such small eyes –
but one is aware of their close concentrated stare
and the amazing way their movements resemble a posse

that turns, just as you are surrounded
by a hundred fish sheriffs, all intent
on preventing your escape on the prairie,
and vanishes to confer over another radio message.

THE SAFE BEACH

Beauty does not swim here. It's utilitarian
that beauty (grown) will take energetic styles
like its own curves: curve calls to curve
the flat safe beach to those whose shapes are mild

and flabby, overflowing, crinkled, run wild
(a means of saying, merely) those who wear
old-fashioned bathing hats and last-minute towels
and converse as though it was a social occasion

since their heads are never in the water as they swim
(if one can call it that). It's not a crawl
or backstroke exactly, more like going to sleep
with gentle arm movements to check the mattress.

SWIMMING WITH THE DEAD WOMAN

In the shelter of a sandbank lay
a still flat-bodiced body under a hat
trimmed with black ribbon. A black mouth
gaped sideways, like a mollusc.

Asleep, we thought, drying ourselves
after our swim. That day the sea

had noticeable cold currents.
The day before sea lettuce

in the lowest waves was crepe
to hang on doors. We swam
in spots as warm as blood
like small rooms or vestibules.

One stroke took us out of them
into chill corridors. They wound
around our feet like ribbons.
'I've swum into a refrigerator,' you called

or at least away from a small town where light
and warmth bubbled underground.
Absurd. But when we saw
the flat chest underneath the hat

not appearing to rise we passed
from another cold spot to the heat
and remarked we'd often seen
black mouths in hospital like that

on sleepers who would tomorrow
breakfast and joke and converse normally
and not know that they talked or gaped
horribly when unconscious.

Last night though both of us searched
the small print in the paper for
'Woman's body discovered on beach'
and an article beginning

'It seems odd with bathers coming and going
some quite close to where she sat...'
and on our next swim, in circles,
you mentioned an anonymous call to the police.

At least, if she was dead, the beach was bare
and it would have been a good way to go:
a commodious basket, drinks, a book
a favourite hat, warm cooling sand.

We hadn't yet discovered how the sea
relates each day to steady heat or wind
not how we expect but according to
its own undoubtedly logical whims.

The dead woman would have given all that
a miss. Perhaps decided the sea was a bad hat
like an errant husband. No really warm depths
until twenty-eight warm days of February.

Then we forgot her, swimming on our backs
the laziest stroke, the most philosophical
the stroke of those carried on a stretcher
DOA, the big toe with the luggage label

and then, facing the shore, we saw her
coming in to bathe. We recognised the nose
outlined in purple zinc, the thin mouth
which closed the cavern. She even had the hat

on until the last minute. She placed it on the sand.
The tide was going out. She weighted it with a stone.
Her chest was flat and hardly rising
but she looked as if she could swim.

Her bony arms splashed water on her shoulders.
As she came closer she called us, 'Ladies'
and called out 'Is it warmer today?'
and 'Are you getting out already?'

Luckily bathing in salt does something to the face
(the reason for total immersion). We looked
we hope, innocent and friendly, praised
the sea and said it was improving

hoped she enjoyed her swim. Lay some moments
in the shallows, always warm, no matter
how gingerly we get in. Does the sea
have this morality to welcome mariners

and castaways, those who summon
faithful eighty-year-old swimmers from their sleep
after being beached and crawling for the sand
and reaching in their bags for hats with bands?

A weekend in the country

Chekhovian perhaps though miniaturised
certainly time enough to ventilate
those shifts of time that make us wise.

Our animation against another kind
certainly watched as we watch out
the house party assembles mentally.

Until we are down to the bleakest of signs
the burning fire, the whipping wind
impulses which we act out utterly.

And in the leisure spaces see them rise
still unabashed, unfertilised
worn down by the country as any country child.

Brutal pruning of a camellia tree

Each winter, so deep and powerful were its roots –
there being an equality between drinking and blooming
like a flush in the cheeks relying on
blood in the ankles – blooms in the coldest days
would press the deep meaning of winter out
and the leaves not as other leaves sustain
these blossoms like a surround of coloured glass.
Now after the professional deed the glass is clear.
Winter falls back into clichés. The bewildered roots
bring the sap to a blind halt, the jewelled hands
are stumped. Likely the powerful heart will send veins
fingers with flower ends, too many flowers out
in superb malfunction first, then settle –
these were the gardener's words – into a proper pessimism.

A white camellia

The most perfect thing
would have no core
but each part be
of core a segment

and not a segment seen
which is division
but like a movement
from room to room

in which a guest
could hardly choose
which bed, which drapes
were better than the rest

and so contented in this flower
feel a possibility
the human heart could follow
petal to thought and thought to petal.

Sputnik and star

One night on Virgil's *Georgics*
my gentle Latin teacher
having volunteered to coach me
after work at the library
we were bending over bees.

I remember I paused rather a lot
since fallen into my hands had come
a superb translation fit for a king
which I would parse with appropriate stumbles
and for these holes secure accolades.

Well this night I had hardly got
into the uncertain swing of it
Virgil and the unseen translator vying
when my teacher's mother without ceremony
hustled us outdoors in the name of history.

Georgics were out. We must look up
and in the firmament of frozen stars
Diogenes in his gaseous barrel
ringed by listeners turned to icicles
detect the ticking passage of a sputnik.

It swam out of the ice I thought
like the eye of a polar bear
something cold and clever and clear

tracking a passage where none had been
a watch held in space by a hair.

My teacher's mother was an old MA
from a distinguished college
one of the first to invade a hall
where the eyes steadily shone
disregarding her progress and her timidity.

For there was something of that in the sputnik I saw
as though its course was not orthodox
not exactly crooked but a kink in the spine
of a girl with stiff boots and long skirt
who sits sidesaddle by a science primer.

I see our three figures at the gate now
and the very night overhead
the old graduand's joy, my teacher's
placating forbearance (she preferred Virgil)
my fatal translation fallen on the floor.

A skyful of stars

Look up and they're word perfect
as you always knew: equations, theorems
the molecular structures like winding stairs
and the explanation of plants, their roots
that may be of air or earth, wherever
the desirable water is, a loving gaze.

Wave over rock

Is this not everything we know
of everything: breakages cost
but are not altogether fatal.

If we stand for a long time
we will be worn down
but our heads will have taken a lot of sea.

For what obscure purpose but
the sea points in, the rock
is the residue of pointing out.

The Feast of All Saints

The napery in heaven's wind
dries and is set down
with candles and unearthly flowers.
Twelve places at each table:
the saints in perfect agape.

Grace can last for hours
and be in a minute over.
They break the bread in slow motion.
The wine freezes in a stream.
Laughter chants around their heads.

He is not coming. It is theirs alone
like a dorm party at midnight.
They clown their roles but cannot spoil their robes.
Whatever they fought with on earth
is removed now: they fight like doves.

Crucifer, thurifer

How good to know these words:
crucifer who carries the crucifix
thurifer the thurible.

Still not broken down:
the cross in procession
the incense in its boat.

One swaying, the other holding.
The skirts of the acolytes
called to create high dignity.

Or at least thurifer creates it
like rosewater, sweet-throwing.
Crucifer brings it, high-headed.

First speech lesson

Sister Teresa bends over me
as I lie with my head on a book
after we've danced to music
articulate gestures, opening the throat.
Poets are sensitive, she says
I've come so I can read better
the upward and downward glide of the voice
the force of the excitor.
At the bottom of my feet the garden
receives the palatals of the rain
and the mute statue of Christ
points to his rib reserve heart.

Behind the mind of a good cliché

Behind the mind of a good cliché
are drawers and drawers of fabric gloves
now only fit for gardening.

Father's favourite saying, mother's was
the bottle of unstoppered perfume
empty among the smalls.

Inter it with tweezers. Behind each line
in burial formation a skull and thighbones
and some fool saluting full of ardour.

Elizabeth Bennet's crossing fields coals of fire trick

Measured by the mud on a petticoat
through layers of clay and carriages
sweep of grasses, the stile's nail
tearing the rent more visible.
Such heart on sleeve, heart on fire stuff
as you draw near to the roaring coals
with wind roses in your cheeks
humbled by the elements and you alone.
If mud be proof of love, if fields
crossed prove... I'd be out of doors
scuttle the carriage by moonlight
lame the horses, secretly skip and walk.

St Paul's kind of love

How does one preserve oneself for it
the kind of gentle not-puffed up
love which endlessly bears
but never swells like a camel
with fat resentment?
Was St Paul thinking of a place
somewhere behind women's hats
where women could take them off
and let their hair stream
in a safe bedroom light?
Did the crusty saint
really have a vision
of two days' delight?

La ligne donnée

The exercise in observation where
several people decide
in their own detail how
a girl going through a door
catches the corner of her dress in it:
La ligne donnée
and what follows
in the altercation that breaks out
Didn't you see how
the skirt swirled, the material being full
how her hand brushed and caused it
one fold shot forward, it was her gait
at once jerky and feminine...

Leave the room at this junction
the poem will follow.

The O in Shakespeare explained

Sometimes a writer turns
his eye to the whole of his subject
or a whole subject apart from it.
O is the word for it.

This book against a stream, a flood
a sky of stars that process
any digression as long as it is large
O is the word for it.

A hundred thousand blades of field
and it held whole in all detail
a wheel of birds that sagas make
O is the word for it.

And Shakespeare's head beginning to ache
for sure the play is a sandwich
and slippery as eel or heart
O is the word for it.

The Veronica's veil technique

Certain that something's happening but what
press a convenient bit of cloth
against the nearest obvious manifestation.
You should come away with a print in your hands
which will be useful later when they're trying to put
a name to it, the event that was unfolding
which you took part in while they only watched.

The Creative Writing Course faces the sonnet

Something formal, say a silver jug
by Cellini or espaliering apples
can be approached by two methods:

usefulness: Cellini was known for spouts
and espaliering apples is practical
in a narrow garden with one wall

or envy: who gave the popes these millions
who left these fossils of great beauty
which still fruit in irony?

A question of gravity

All day we fought against the sky
and in theatres aimed towards the gods
spun on our toes our eyes high on a wall
above gravity addressed our purest thoughts.

All night we lay weakly giving in
held someone close if someone was around
murmured a prayer and looked towards the roof
dreamed and straightened out our backs.

Margo lecturing on death

Death to her blond hair is stone to air
but air sustains and stone can melt
'If the world ends I shall not play with rocks
or sit by the roadside making cairns.'
Prepare first (Margo has for weeks)

to allow beauty one hair's width
out of death's reason and his hour
which she has this afternoon defeated.

Stubble fields

In some stubble fields an indentation
perhaps a small swamp dried in summer
traces a faint black imperfect sowing
like a panda's eye.

Fields that contain these small infelicities
are more beautiful than the perfect
skinhead fields they emulate
more individual, with a love-bite.

Punk girl sketching the Parthenon frieze

In flowing black, down to black boots hard as stone
but hairless, shaven, like a gold-glowing dome
and one earring and one twinkling stud
in each nostril she sits sketching
part of the drapes of the wall of frieze.

In the distance the torso of Iris agrees
a head's an inessential. Her carved clothes
rush against her body during flight
though hide the lightest beating of a heart.
Two headless creatures are making a sketch.

A cortège of daughters

A quite ordinary funeral: the corpse
unknown to the priest. The twenty-third psalm.
The readings by serious businessmen
one who nearly tripped on the unaccustomed pew.
The kneelers and the sitters like sheep and goats.

But by some prior determination a row
of daughters and daughters-in-law rose
to act as pallbearers instead of men
all of even height and beautiful.
One wore in her hair a black and white striped bow.

And in the midst of their queenliness
one in dark flowered silk, the corpse
had become a man before they reached the porch
so loved he had his own dark barge
which their slow moving steps rowed
as a dark lake is sometimes surrounded by irises.

Saints' names

Each letter from my friend is headed
with a saint's name. For December
she elects between St John Damascene
St Jane Frances, St Thomas Beckett.

A vast dictionary, I imagine, sits before her
with no vacant feast days. Sometimes
she strikes an obligation marked in red:
all the Fridays in Lent, the Assumption of the BVM

But most pleasing are the obscure saints
with odd spellings: St Bernadette Soubirous
St Fidelis of Sigmaringa, Sts Charles Lwanga & Companions
and an especial favourite: St Polycarp.

What have they in common: St Peter Chrysologus
St Ignatius of Loyola: two she will never use
in the same year as they sit side by side
as even St Teresa of Avila took mass only on Sundays?

I think it is euphony. Or a comment.
What small trials today compare to St Xystus II?
Or pictures: Sts Pontian & Hippolytus
a holy hippopotamus under a bridge

or being noticeably well-mannered
for such elect company where simplicity
might have been expected, even nicknames:
St Maximillian Kolbe, St John Chrysostom.

A small seascape in oils

Instead of fruit, furniture or flesh
squall, cloudburst and stain
are the seascape accoutrements.

Squall is a window, cloudburst the action
in still life seen in wrung-neck fowls
or limp rabbits hung up by their feet.

Stain and shadow are the flesh tints
waves wear to delineate their form
the way nudes bend to pick up their shoes.

6 little poems about Canada

LITTLE CANADIAN HOUSES

Stoically, white-foreheaded, thin-lipped
they resist the plain, although they're in a street
their moral figures that never grew thick
their locket at the throat embellishments
would press out such a style you'd think
into prose and verse and sweep the leaves.

A GARLAND OF SWEET GRASS FROM THE INDIAN RESERVATION

Nestled in the box of brutal gifts
shiny brochures, plans and culture bids
when on the walls you're forced into our dress
waistcoated chiefs, even your wedding dress
this plaited ring, waist-size or noose
crosses the earth on silent moccasins.

NIAGARA FALLS

If Keats's Grecian urn had to pour
in solemn stillness, one-less-large
than spirit which is small
this would be the next gradation:
silent watchers at a huge waterfall.

SQUIRREL

What is punctuating the leaves
with phrasing, accents *aigus* and *graves*
and writing underneath the notes
of joining quick first drafts with strokes
that connect the grammar to the tail?

WHY DO COLONIAL VOICES RISE ON THE LAST WORD?

A disbelief that rushes to believe
that you will disbelieve we believe
and that we should be doubtful in belief
does not unsettle belief underneath.

WALKING IN MAPLE LEAVES

All the books we left open
or fell into sleep reading
we are punished by walking over and remembering.

The lost pages spread out for our eyes.
Sometimes they are buried in drifts
or move a little, with the effort of waiting.

Nine postcards on a wall

Balancing on Mrs James Cook's bonnet
is Edouard Manet looking bored
Colette with paper roses below the Magi
Dickens' house beside the Delphi charioteer
Turner beside a lady in a picadill
and red buses going round the square.

Details when you list them can cross borders
into the next postcard; often they join
in some kind of espérance, or forlorn
cast their looks towards each other in the mist.
They could have quite a party in the house of Dickens
all but the charioteer arriving by bus.

Error on a quiz programme

'Give me the names of three lady violinists
who lived at Haworth Parsonage?'
Charlotte on the violin, Anne the viola
and Emily on the violoncello.
Each evening in the dark drawing room
they drew up their instruments and played
with the wind above the graves.

Charlotte was most in demand as a soloist.
Anne was too shy and with a limited repertoire.
The violoncello takes up too much room in a carriage.
If anyone was asked out it was usually Charlotte.
Emily carried the violoncello on her back
as she tramped the moors. Sometimes
she laid it across a stream and jumped over it.

The muse (for women poets)

I often think of him
as secretly booked into the Algonquin
and sending up the bellboy
with flowers and a knowing grin.

'The gent's anonymous.' His tip
outdoes yours for information.
Coming down the lift is rosy
and what is this light about the page?

The French translation

'Did you get a nurse and an ambulance?'
I was slightly better at it and with insight
had unravelled a rather boring landscape description
a word I took for bracken, a stream in its midst
but no accident requiring medical intervention.

What to say? 'I may quite well be wrong.'
In the bracken lay the body of our French mistress
and her black bicycle with its basket wrecked.
Across the river murmurous sounds that grew
and nearby, what we agreed on, *un lapin*.

The ha-ha

Hardly noticed, though we set out to see
where the lawn apparently never ended
in 'a ditch not seen, a sunken fence'.

The ha-ha. Someone, bending, invisibly
was chopping wood. A hum below the ground
an autumn day, below the lawn, disclosed

but not a scene normally to write about.
Just the view preserved by stealth
and all its workings out of sight.

For someone riding by or running in fright
a sudden leap as the world came up
an ancient belief carefully set out

by weeks of digging and planting like a trap
the approaches with careless lushness
as if the world should end in spume.

'You saw the ha-ha?' as we came in.
We did but instead of praising said
it made us look up at the clouds.

A flight of starlings

A shape between a fish or star
turns over houses, over trees
with effort, effort written large.

Who said that day could easily end
or migration be a pure instinct
has not looked or felt its beats.

The pain is in it but a heart
is larger still and is the shape
behind the effort that they make.

The sea question

The sea asks 'How is your life now?'
It does so obliquely, changing colour.
It is never the same on any two visits.

It is never the same in any particular
only in generalities: tide and such matters
wave height and suction, pebbles that rattle.

It doesn't presume to wear a white coat
but it questions you like a psychologist
as you walk beside it on its long couch.

The butterfly girl

Her unblemished skin thick with pancake
like wing dust, she asks me if I know
the meaning of 'butterflies' in dreams.

How light sometimes a librarian's footsteps
to the small reference section of the arcane
and quick through the index to *Dreams*.

Butterflies = to fluctuate I explain
wondering how she will interpret this:
as fate unkind or rising like a sea?

Soon we are bending over the hugest Dictionary
and I am making sea-motions with my hands
'Your fate will ebb and flow, it sounds hopeful

some things will go well, some less so
but butterflies in dreams are not threatening
even the Oxford English Dictionary says so.'

Effleurage

Zephyr over water (the last move
of zephyr outside a zoo)
so light, unseen-to-move
a liquid stroke over liquid beneath.

Skin could do this to skin
and find fish within
or heavier breathing aggrieved bears
without ice holes to speak.

Stay, the moving fingers semaphore
to bear or maggot, herring or swan
pushing their snouts towards us.
Touch is our deepest theology.

A few words from old postcards

It's dark at 4.30 pm. That's your
London cum continent trip in 1996.
I raise a glass to you. Paris, outdoors.
The latest kind of snow-resisting lamps.

Just come from evensong in the Abbey.
(Bath). You were descending through
layers of tourism to antiquarian books and textiles
If this sounds choleric I have a raging 'flu.

The British Library is efficient but not beautiful.
Your red scarf wraps your shoulders like a cloak.
*Anxiety is simply us trying to control events
from a distance.* Head bowed, I see you writing it.

The moon

'If you have time tonight' says the TV hostess
'Look at the moon. It's full and particularly
beautiful.' So I do. After preparing

a meal and washing the dishes, settling
myself for evening I pay a call
from my front door on the moon.

There is nothing I can say to it. A circle
forms in my mouth which remains closed.
A cavernous disc closes my throat

or my neck is elongated by a stack
of tight silver rings. So bright is the moon
I hardly dare decipher the legend imprinted on it.

A rabbit? A hare? Something in profile
or declivities, ranges and valleys
dried river beds, craters? No design

can mar its beauty, like touching a soft
cheek in the dark, feeling a profile
looking ahead, but watching.

Encounter with Honore

Tiny aged Frenchwoman encountered
at a party where in your corner
of the window seat between forty winks
you received those who attempted French.

'Je...' one began and waved her hands
in a Gallic gesture. 'Je regrette que...'
You smiled like a knowing concierge
and waited. Not one English word ever

escaped your lips. 'Bonjour, madame,' I said
quickly passing through the morning parlour
where your croissant and confiture were laid
with a pretty napkin and a flower

and then, as evening fell, 'Bonsoir.'
But on the last day I attempted
what, I think, caused you horreur
a quick kiss on both cheeks

hands on your tiny low shoulders
and, preceding it, a little speech
coached and accompanied by one fluent
'Madame, je vous en prie...' and 'Au revoir.'

To Finn, before he walks

Days, hours, perhaps mere minutes before
standing firmly, one hand braced, one free
to point or balance or gesture or conduct
your step will come and who will see it?

And after you have stepped and fallen
got up, and decided to step is better
and falling will falter, and on and on
the steps will come and run together

until the years like gates are stepped through
and the days like doors, the weeks
and everything opens: a tread
makes arches, altars, entrances.

Son surviving a car crash

Cecilia Bartoli sings in the living room.
The brandy balloon with its brandy and milk
invites the reverent handling of a chalice.

O clear alchemic warbling as if
a soul might tug on a string and stay
glass empty of its libation and milky.

Over the white bedcover and sheets comes
the idea of angel wings, the force
of heavenly persuasion, the escape

through so many competing jostling atoms
the path opening at your feet, the few scratches
your bewildered subdued voice on the phone.

Reading a collection of poems marked by a previous reader

Angrily I take out the soft honey-coloured rubber
and leave crumbs on the pages where
rhymes are circled and margin comments
and, once, an inferior imitating poem.

Who has needed to explain these poems
with underlinings? Not Mary Oliver*
who wrote them, taking into account
the spaces and the space around the spaces.

* Mary Oliver: *New and Selected Poems*, 1992

The Oxford comma

A little knot of writers at a
prize-giving ceremony, standing
uncertainly, looking at the stage

and the side table with scrolls and envelopes
containing magical cheques, we discuss
to show erudition and hide fear

the Oxford comma and the use of it.
'Unnecessary,' someone offers. 'An extra
fence where no animal was escaping.'

'But perhaps a breath,' another suggests.
'A large egalitarian family being given pocket money
or sharing beds, a demarcation with bolsters.'

Victory, loss, effusions, and stoicism
someone thinks but doesn't say
as the crowd files in and takes their seats.

Rainbow

It appears, it is there, like something
emanating from an emotional source
or a complicated chemical reaction:

here are the colours, red, orange, yellow...
just now fixed: the sky is the developing tank
and the promise hangs there, suspended

by invisible pegs. It will not stay long:
the coming into being, the becoming
if anyone notices it, fortuitously, its message

is to take from it whatever significance
seems appropriate: a promise with a
time-frame, a statute of limitations.

Suffolk sheep

Like cold white winter hands clothed
in black gloves: the black faces
the white bodies, the green fields

how strong beauty is: how compactly
assembled: the first day of gloves
taking them out of the drawer, feeling

the wool part and warm as the fingers
slide into their compartments and the thumb
gets special treatment. The Suffolk sheep

have always got special treatment. Design
excellence: the dark dainty heads compressed
in dark veils, the beauty of those cropping jawbones.

To a friend with osteoporosis

I think of you in this warmer century
walking in cold stone halls and walls
coming to a vast fireplace from which
little heat issues over trampled straw.

I think of you walking in a long cloak
by a pond from which birds rise
into cold unprotective bare trees
and I wish hot water could be put into

rings on your fingers and a locket at your throat
like the Medicis who put poison into
rings which they surreptitiously opened
over goblets filled with insidious wine.

Walking a newborn child

Along the passage, slightly rocking
holding the hard jerking head with my hand
trying to still the cries and the butting
and begin the whisper of a lullaby

like a faint note in the harsh cry
the way the head plunges, the face engorges
and yet an arm seems almost asleep
flung into the air like a piece of statuary.

Ten times I walk the short passage and turn
and walk to the room where the cradle hangs
like a vast zeppelin, an impossible dream
hung with mosquito netting like a nebula.

A pattern of marching

Armies when they marched had men
at least two who could tell
the marching patterns of the army they opposed
by putting their ear(s) to the ground.

Stillness behind and these two lying down
a hand held up to halt but miles away
(two was the distance they were supposed
to detect) the other army went marching on.

A certain quantity of men, a certain vibration
carried to a certain depth which was unease
poachers in these regions went undetected
courting couples in the hedgerows undisturbed.

Perhaps near nightfall was the best time to hear it
sound carries better and to bivouac
spurs the last hours of marching
the rhythm, established, would be second nature

and as hard to stop as any train.
Later it would be trains most men could hear
running on their grooves like any record player
a skilled performance anyone could share.

Pansies

Some blindness they face into asks for touch
as Jane Eyre asked Mr Rochester
to memorise her face and grant her that
smoke would do as well as blackener.

Indeed he thought Jane's brow so conscience struck
its lines so fine, her heart so well enclosed
might not her eyes have wished the grief of fire
to free these great dark shadows which the pansies have.

To Joseph, in hospital

Nothing can ever cross
from the well to the poorly
except flowers, confectionery
other items of burglary.

Between men and angels
the gap is not so great
as those with injections
and bringers of grapes

Just lie and endure it.
Time heals and it waits
to give the weak callisthenics
and the strong second thoughts.

Heights

Here are our garden trees at night
stirred by wind but not stirred in their roots
or they seem noticeably aloof
the wind is higher, quite another height.

Not the height of planes that level out
above all weather, above reproof
though their passengers may shiver
and press a bell for blankets or a pillow.

The wind between these has a place to sport
(at least tonight). It sends its ripples down
like streamers from a ship that's leaving port
for deep patched sea that sinks like continents.

A little town, at night, from the air

A boxing ring. That's what the main street makes
rising on its yellow lights to make rope rings
around the other recessed silver streets.

A little square town behind whose lights
who knows how many boxing matches
are occurring, how many rooms of raised tempo

translated to the town's whole terrain
perfectly square but the gold ropes floating
the elevated hopes and borders.

Only as we come closer, the town coming
under our wing, do we see
the central important street settle

back and become a boxer's belt
something that gleams like a river
the lights dividing to make an avenue.

Rhyme, unrhyme

A deliberate village where history is stilled
chairs rock, swings on verandahs filled
with twosomes, the deep-shuttered dark
burns with poetry but never leaves a mark.

In some dust siding, on the illicit train
stowaways hide from the landscape, endlessly plain
and space their conversation, spit and play some notes
and if it rhymes it takes away all their hopes.

A small potato crop

In the tiny square garden
– handkerchief-size transferred to earth –
my gloved hand touches – earth gloves
thicker as the garden is wide –
small white clear shapes of a potato crop.

They come from the soil not
as I had imagined, drawn
from mire to air, like a potato birth
but clear, almost jokingly, jovial
as though they bounced up, fair

as a clutch of yellow-haired girls
who have been playing in pinafores
before a photograph and fallen into
the developing fluid; the sort of dirty
called 'clean dirt', noble, upright

a blemish on otherwise faultless humans
or shoes polished like a guardsman's
that receive the splatter of horses' hooves
under which baptism of fire and water
it is possible to see their morals gleaming.

Re-reading Stephen Spender

Someone, since I last took it out
has borrowed these poems and appended
small initials to the endings
sometimes N and sometimes G.

Does N mean No and G mean Good
or N mean nice, easily understood?
Could G be grandiose, grave or gaudy?
No key is offered, none given.

It disturbs my re-reading of Stephen Spender
to have these letters attached like fish hooks
on last lines: *The map of everywhere we'd been* N
I'm haunted by their emptiness G.

Eating chocolates

In their box, laid out like a maze
the chocolates reveal themselves to our gaze
and touch. Mock-electrified we approach
a fingertip, hover, consider each throat

a vampire might bend over before assaying
two incisors to puncture. Some saying
they prefer hard but cannot squeeze
take a chance, bite and sneeze

'It's ginger!' the one flavour they abhor.
Others with peppermint, praline, violet or
rum truffle, fudge whirl, simple speak
while the case shatters and the contents leak

to those who've unwisely chosen rocks.
The ceiling falls but then a shock
as though they dined on jewels or pearls
like émigrés or White Russian girls

who instead of cyanide have strapped
to a molar an heirloom. Trapped
at the border they will swallow
or cash it later for a dollar.

The servants' quarters in Queen Mary's dolls house

How well the plain wears.
The butler's room seems so
desirable beside the Queen's.

The regulation parlourmaid's
mattress though thin
is posture-pedic on its wires

and not half as dusty as the King's
nightly tossings in a turret
of high dust curtains and crown

a room a Queen would fear to enter
without appointment. Imagine
the closed curtains parting

perhaps in the middle of a dream.
Oh, it's only you, the Queen.
Come in and share the blanket

which on the butler's bed
is fastened with a pin
perfectly proportioned, like the stitches.

How hard to arrange chaise longue
escritoire, night cabinet
to look informal in a room

the size of a cathedral vestibule
or to lower the ceiling
with huge portraits over fireplaces.

Only the servants' quarters to which
they climbed, with trouser press
and floral jug, look neat

and gentle as an hour off
to rest the feet, open a book
and lie beneath the coverlet.

Putting one's head in a blossoming tree

Spectacular through the glass, awesome in air
still you suggest I come closer still
and put my head under the flowering plum.

Under and within. A hat one wears and looks at
feeling the flattering of the brim and above
the crown, its patterning unstinted and rare.

It makes me think a head of hair exists
only for ornament or spring air
still in this place to concentrate.

A small ordered garden on a disordered planet

Prim as the borders are
there is no credit from the air
where the spaceship looks on bands
whose tiniest plots approximate
to a stream they call the flux.

The basket and the trowel are hid
likewise the costume and the gloves
the rose is self-picking
when staked and grown
it leads to a room and not a world.

But if each far-seeing band comprises
the dominant elements that are around
the falling of a petal may
drive a mauve to ground
or make the band an Amazon.

Jennifer's wedding

Catch a glimpse of her, super secretary
walking white between the ilexes
towards the sunk-in-sun rose garden.

Here the whole heat of afternoon
stupefies and the panama hats
of the groom and groomsman ward off

it seems the roses' radar scent.
Deep through the archway glows the table
with its rich cloth and scented posy

where the rose garden will write
the events superimposed on it
the rings' brief flashing, the whitened grins

the motionless leaves of heavy trees
to which a wedding is not even one spin
in a year's ring, a mille-feuille of growing.

Sitting in Margo's garden reading Philippe Ariès' *The Hour of our Death*

Every visit I take it from the bookcase
where it lies on its side with leaves inside
pressed between the cover and the frontispiece

leaves as brown and dry as old bones
and sharp with the spite of death. I turn
the familiar pages and read the headings:

The Tame Death, The Death of the Self
as if all history were portending
to a revision, deeper than deeds.

The Age of the Beautiful Death, complete
acceptance or evasion, like two continents
in opposite hemispheres. Here, the Catacombs

of the Capuchin Convent, Palermo: the odd choir
that has just shuffled in to fill the stalls
and here, in domestic Montpelier, Vermont

the funerary sculpture of Little Margaret, white
and pure. How could those skulls, if Margaret dug
undo her marzipan purity? Look, she might

say, running with one as a vessel. What use
can we put this to? What use is death?
And our attitudes to it, do they

alter, in any respect, the angel, or just
the way we look at him? Those often-
elevated floor slabs of churches

hiding corruption in a blaze of lead and glass
or the quiet New England burial ground
of graves like gentle sheep, cropping together

in a meadow that seems more eternal
than their eliding inscriptions. *The Dead Body.*
The Visit to the Cemetery. I close my eyes

then open them to look up at the sky
then the treetops, the climbing sweet peas
the pond with lilies, the cat's grave

commemorated by a little stone wall
and a fresh tussi-mussi picked that day.
Between swooning and fright

between the heartsick knight and the hospice
between the neurological bright light
I close the book I love like a tablet.

Listening to *The Goldberg Variations*

A dream of piano playing: I would rise
from a long disagreeable dinner party
where some had been insulted, some ignored
(I was of the ignored, the cheek turned aside

the gaze downward, the heart raw)
when someone opposite, a gentleman in tails
would whisper low or pass a note
Do you like hearing the piano played?

Quietly we rose and slipped through the door
until, several doors dividing, where
the air grew quiet and sounds faded
stood a venerable piano with a candle sconce

at which the gentleman seated himself
with (first smile of the night) a flick of tails
a shooting of cuffs, a conspiratorial look
and began to play *The Goldberg Variations.*

On the polished floor I sat in evening dress
slipped off my sandals and my elbow gloves
rested my head against a piano leg
and let all varieties of grief and love

flow into resolution and a method
for is not life of stairs composed
of climbing melody and deep repose
and this minute by minute's easing

as the white hands with their little hairs
on second knuckles rose and tried
to slip between the keys until
a smile, about the time of *Quodlibet,*

accrued. In the distance chairs were held
and scaped back and napkins tossed down.
'Who cares they've gone?' some brute said
as the last notes brought their solace like a plate

and the gentleman in tails got up and snuffed
out the candle between a third finger and a thumb.
I rose too, stiff and resolved, and walked
through the door that opened on the street.

ELIZABETH SMITHER was born in New Plymouth, New Zealand in 1941. Her first collection of poems, *Here come the clouds*, appeared in 1975. Since then, she has brought out ten collections, including the prize-winning *A Pattern of Marching* (New Zealand Book Awards 1990) and *The Lark Quartet* (Montana New Zealand Book Awards 2000), both from Auckland University Press.

Her poems have been widely published in Australia, Canada, Britain and America. She has also written short stories and novels, her latest short story collection, *Listening to the Everly Brothers* (Penguin) appearing in 2002 and a novel, *The sea between us* (also from Penguin), in 2003.

Her most recent collection of poems, *Red Shoes*, (Godwit, 2003) was the result of her two-year term as Te Mata New Zealand poet laureate.

This is her first full-length collection to be published in the UK.

Also available in the
ARC PUBLICATIONS
International Poets series

LOUIS ARMAND (Australia)
Inexorable Weather

DON COLES (Canada)
Someone has Stayed in Stockholm

SARAH DAY (Australia)
New & Selected Poems

GAIL DENDY (South Africa)
Painting the Bamboo Tree

KATHERINE GALLAGHER (Australia)
Tigers on the Silk Road

ROBERT GRAY (Australia)
Lineations

MICHAEL S. HARPER (U.S.A)
Selected Poems

ALAMGIR HASHMI (Pakistan)
The Ramazan Libation

DENNIS HASKELL (Australia)
Samuel Johnson in Marrickville

DINAH HAWKEN (New Zealand)
Small Stories of Devotion

BRIAN HENRY (U.S.A.)
Astronaut
Graft

RICHARD HOWARD (U.S.A.)
Trappings

ANDREW JOHNSTON (New Zealand)
The Open Window

JOHN KINSELLA (Australia)
Lightning Tree
The Silo:
A PASTORAL SYMPHONY
The Undertow:
NEW & SELECTED POEMS
Landbridge:
ANTHOLOGY OF CONTEMPORARY AUSTRALIAN POETRY
ED. JOHN KINSELLA

ANTHONY LAWRENCE (Australia)
Strategies for Confronting Fear
NEW & SELECTED POEMS

THOMAS LUX (U.S.A.)
The Street of Clocks

J.D.McCLATCHY (U.S.A.)
Division of Spoils

MARY JO SALTER (U.S.A.)
A Kiss in Space

ANDREW SANT (Australia)
The Unmapped Page

C. K. STEAD (New Zealand)
Dog

ANDREW TAYLOR (Australia)
The Stone Threshold

JOHN TRANTER (Australia)
The Floor of Heaven